CLIP ART

FOR YEAR B

STEVE ERSPAMER, SM

LTP

LITURGY
TRAINING
PUBLICATIONS

Duplicating the Art in this Book

The art in this book may be duplicated freely by the
purchaser for use in a parish, school, community,
or other institution. This art may not be used on any
materials that are intended to be sold.

Clip Art for Year B © 1993, Archdiocese of Chicago:
Liturgy Training Publications, 3949 South Racine Avenue,
Chicago IL 60609; 1-800-933-1800; orders@ltp.org;
fax 1-800-933-7094. All rights reserved. See our website
at www.LTP.org.

Printed in the United States of America.

16   15   14   13   12   8   9   10   11   12

ISBN 978-1-56854-009-2

CLIPB

Table of Contents

Introduction

Opening this book is much like entering a great cathedral: Everywhere one turns, the great mysteries of the faith, the holy men and women of our tradition, and the symbols that have conveyed Christian hopes and beliefs from one generation to the next catch the eye, delight the heart and engage the mind. This book contains hundreds of delightful, engaging illustrations useful for bulletins, worship folders, calendars and handouts for each season and Sunday of the liturgical year.

About the Artist and the Art

Steve Erspamer is a Marianist brother who resides in St. Louis, Missouri. He is a many-faceted artist who works in clay, stone, fresco, art glass, silkscreened fabrics, block prints and, as this book demonstrates, cut paper. Steve studied at St Mary's University in San Antonio, Texas; the Art Institute of San Antonio; Creighton University in Omaha; and Boston University. He has traveled in Western Europe and in India as a student of sacred art.

The artist brings to this book a respect for traditional iconography. In the positioning of the figures of Mary and the angel Gabriel, in the depicting of a parable, even in the drawing of an apple, there are customary styles in Christian tradition. These forms have evolved, in part, because of their beauty and elegance, but also, in part, as expressions of the gospel and as emblems of the reign of God.

Many of the images in this book have been drawn in the style of stone carvings in the Romanesque churches that dot the great medieval pilgrimage route through France and Spain. This style, in turn, borrows from Byzantine iconography. As examples of this style, incidental characters often are pictured smaller than main characters; disciples show their allegiance to Jesus by bowing; sometimes a figure will bend and twist to fit a form.

Decoration sometimes adds another layer of meaning— tame animals suggest a return to paradise; wild animals suggest the Spirit's gift of fortitude; roses are signs of the flowering of God's reign; pomegranates represent the fruitfulness of the kingdom of heaven.

Throughout this book on the pages facing the art are brief statements about the art. The Sunday's or feast's calendar date is included here. The scriptures of the Mass are listed.

Illustrations of the Sunday Readings

The book of scriptures read at the eucharist—the lectionary—is organized according to a few principles:

The first readings are most often from the books of Jewish scriptures, what Christians call the Old Testament. But during Eastertime the first readings are from the Acts of the Apostles.

Second readings are read in sequence through Ordinary Time. From the Second to the Sixth Sunday of Year B, we hear First Corinthians; from the Seventh to the Fourteenth Sunday, Second Corinthians; from the Fifteenth to the Twenty-first Sunday, Ephesians; from the Twenty-second to the Twenty-sixth Sunday, James; from the Twenty-seventh to the Thirty-third Sunday, Hebrews. During the Easter season this year, the second readings are taken from First John.

Sunday gospels in Year B are most often from Mark, but from the Seventeenth to the Twenty-first Sunday in Ordinary Time, on the Third, Fourth and Fifth Sundays of Lent, and on most of the Sundays of Easter, the gospels are taken from John.

In this book, all the first readings and gospel readings of Year B have been illustrated. Illustrations for the second readings are here, too, but they may take a bit of searching to find. For the second readings, a single piece of art can sometimes be used several Sundays in a row. The index can help you locate appropriate art for the second readings.

Uses for This Art

Each season of the year receives a full-page illustration suitable for covers of bulletins or seasonal worship aids. They also can be reproduced for children to color, or enlarged to use as posters.

The supplemental designs and images found throughout this book—images from nature, saints or an image from the Sunday psalm—can be used for a variety of parish, school and home events: confirmation, first communion, pancake breakfasts, potluck suppers, back-to-school announcements, invitations, birth announcements, concert programs and more.

Preparing a Handout

Communications have become more visual and less verbal. Perhaps as a result of television, people are accustomed to complex visuals. They know when something looks unprofessional. That means that all of us who prepare parish bulletins, worship programs and the like are expected to produce sophisticated publications. That's hard work. It's skilled work, too, and it requires a sense of playfulness and creativity to do it well.

Here are a few hints: Allow yourself plenty of time to work on your project. Do the work as soon as you have all the necessary information; don't wait until the last minute. Something always go awry: The copier needs toner, you run out of tape, you can't find a certain piece of music. Spare yourself some headaches.

Assemble your materials: Scissors, paper, tape or glue stick or wax stick (wax allows you to move pieces easily), ruler (a clear, flexible ruler with a grid marked on it is invaluable for laying things out straight).

Word processors are a great help in producing nice-looking publications, especially with the aid of a good printer. Try not to mix typefaces; different sizes or degrees of boldness of the same typeface can be used instead. Rather than using the title of a song as it is printed with the music, key in the title and the copyright notices in the same typeface as the rest of the program. (If you use a lot of music from one publisher, create a macro for that publisher's copyright notice. Include your reprint license number, if you have one.) Don't forget to include page numbers.

Be careful when mixing styles of art; it's hard to do this well, and you may achieve a more professional look if you stick to one style. Be sure that all your pieces of art are clean and clear. Use correction fluid to get rid of any speckles, or find a clean copy.

Use "white space" liberally—not every corner of a handout should be filled. Make sure both words and art have adequate space around them to give a clean look to the handout. Take a second look at the appropriateness of the art. Proofread your work, and have someone else proofread it as well.

Investigate using unusual ink colors and papers; printers are happy to help, but be sure to ask about the extra cost, particularly of colored inks. When you choose ink and paper colors, remember that readability is the most important concern. There should be enough contrast between the ink and the paper to allow everyone to read the words, and the two colors together shouldn't make the eye "pop."

Emphasize the liturgical calendar in the parish bulletin, even if at times that means being at odds with other calendars. That might mean that Mother's Day gets a bit less attention than the season of Easter, that Valentine's Day gets no notice in years it falls right at the beginning of Lent, that during Advent the bulletin is free of Christmas images, and that the bulletin keeps up the Christmas spirit even if the shops have called it quits.

Be conservative with words and liberal with art. For example, a worship folder cover need not state the obvious—"Christmas," "Lent"—but be aware that these sometimes serve as mementos of special occasions. For anniversaries, ordinations, funerals, weddings or such events, include the names of the principal persons involved and the date somewhere in the bulletin, but not necessarily on the cover.

Enlarge and reduce this art as needed. Many photocopiers can do this. The art in this book was fashioned from cut paper, which lends itself to the production of crisp enlargements and reductions. There is a point of diminishing returns, however: Be careful that the art is not reduced so much that it becomes undecipherable.

When preparing worship folders, try to enlarge words and music where appropriate—this can invite participation. Don't be afraid to make items as big as possible, as long as the whole is in scale.

You are free to copy the art in this book without acknowledgments if you use the art for a parish, a school or other institution. However, you may not use this art (or any clip art) without written permission from the publisher if you sell the reproduction.

If you use a great deal of the art in this book through the year, please, at times, acknowledge the artist, the name of the book and the publisher. Users of parish and school handouts will appreciate the information. You may also consider, on occasion, providing explanations of the art you reproduce. Often it's helpful to call attention to art and, at times, to explain images that may be unfamiliar.

Liturgical images can educate as well as illustrate. They teach without words. They tell stories, evoke moods, and remind us of things we almost forgot. The images in this book do even more: They can lead us into the lectionary, into the scriptures and psalms and even the spirit of the liturgy. They can lead us into mystery.

Works of art,
the most exalted expressions of the human spirit,
bring us closer and closer
to the divine Artisan.

—*Paul VI, 1971*

Christ is the image of the invisible God,
the firstborn of all creation.

—*Colossians 1:15*

The arts, by their very nature,
are oriented toward the infinite beauty of God,
which they attempt in some way to portray
by the work of human hands.

—*Constitution on the Sacred Liturgy, #122*

The church has a need of saints, yes,
but also of artists,
of skilled and good artists.
Both saints and artists are a witness
of the living Spirit of Christ.

—*Paul VI, 1967*

The liturgy must be human as well as divine.
It should have participation and it should have art.

—*Reynold Hillenbrand, 1962*

Advent Bulletin Cover

Advent lasts from the fourth Sunday before Christmas until the evening of Christmas Eve.

About the art: "A shoot shall sprout from the stump of Jesse," Isaiah tells us. From the house of Jesse of Bethlehem, God chose the one who was to be king of Israel, David, the youngest of Jesse's seven sons. Through David, Jesse is the ancestor of Jesus. The Jesse tree is a traditional image found in mosaics and windows. Many of these images are very ornate, with branches depicting Jesus' ancestors and various prophets and other biblical figures. If there is such an image in your church, draw attention to it in the bulletin during Advent.

ADVENT

First Sunday of Advent

violet

Isaiah 63:16b—17, 19b; 64:2—7
  Psalm 63
1 Corinthians 1:3—9
Mark 13:33—37

About the art: Today's readings remind us that we are the work of God's hands and that we always should be prepared to meet God by keeping alert, by offering thanks, by using the gifts we have been given.

Art for the Solemnity of the Immaculate Conception is on pages 4 and 6.

Second Sunday of Advent

violet

Isaiah 40:1–5, 9–11
   Psalm 85
2 Peter 3:8–14
Mark 1:1–8

About the art: John the Baptist appears this week for the first time, exhorting us to repent, to make ready for the Lord, who will come like a thief in the night. This less-than-comforting image is juxtaposed with the image of a God who is like a shepherd. In the land whose people fear the Lord, Psalm 85 tells us, truth and kindness shall meet, justice and peace shall kiss, truth will spring out of the earth and justice will look down from heaven.

The border of stars recalls the December sky and looks forward to the star of Bethlehem.

Other images of John the Baptist can be found on pages 5, 14 and 51.

4

Immaculate Conception

white

Genesis 3:9–15, 20
  Psalm 98
Ephesians 1:3–6, 11–12
Luke 1:26–38

About the art: This feast celebrates Mary, through whom the human race cooperated with God in overcoming sin, which came into the world when we cooperated with the serpent. All creation sings joyfully of the wonders that God has done for us.

Another illustration of today's gospel can be found on page 6. Other images of Adam and Eve are found on pages 34, 48 and 71.

Third Sunday of Advent

rose or violet

Isaiah 61:1–2a, 10–11
  Magnificat (Luke 1:46–48, 49–50, 53–54)
  1 Thessalonians 5:16–24
John 1:6–8, 19–28

About the art: Many images of the reign of God pour out of the scriptures for today: a robe of salvation, a bride and groom adorned in their finery, a captive set free, the earth bringing forth life. It was this reign that John the Baptist preached. Paul exhorts us not to stifle the spirit.

The Third Sunday of Advent was once called Gaudete (Rejoice) Sunday, from the first word of the entrance antiphon for the day: "Rejoice in the Lord always; again I say, rejoice! The Lord is near" (Philippians 4:4, 5). In some parishes the customary rose-colored vestments are worn, and the Advent wreath may include a rose candle among the purple ones. The bulletin or other handouts may make use of this color.

Fourth Sunday of Advent

violet

2 Samuel 7:1–5, 8b–12, 14a, 16
  Psalm 89
Romans 16:25–27
Luke 1:26–38

About the art: Through Nathan, David learns that it will not be his work to build a house for the Lord, but he also learns that the Lord promises to be with Israel always and to maintain the house of David forever. Mary, betrothed to Joseph of the House of David, hears the word of the Lord and conceives the one whom all the prophets foretold. Another image of the Annunciation appears on page 4.

In the final week of Advent, we turn our eyes toward Bethlehem. In many Hispanic communities, the journey of Mary and Joseph to Bethlehem is celebrated with *Las Posadas,* a procession from house to house, looking for a place for the Christ Child to be born. This is celebrated with music and food and great merriment.

This is the last opportunity to print the Christmas schedule. Even if you've printed it before now, some people are sure to have lost it or never to have seen it. Reprinting it may save a lot of phone calls.

Christmas Season Bulletin Cover

The Christmas season lasts from the evening of Christmas Eve until the feast of the Baptism of the Lord.

About the art: All the days of Christmas—the Nativity, the Holy Family, the Motherhood of Mary, the Epiphany, the Baptism of the Lord, the various saints and martyrs whom we recall—celebrate the incarnation, God's taking on human flesh in Jesus, and Jesus' continuing presence in the world through his people. The parish bulletin can help the parish keep all of Christmas.

CHRISTMAS TIME

8

Christmas Day

white

Vigil

Isaiah 62:1–5
  Psalm 89
Acts 13:16–17, 22–25
Matthew 1:1–25

Night

Isaiah 9:1–6
  Psalm 96
Titus 2:11–14
Luke 2:1–14

Dawn

Isaiah 62:11–12
  Psalm 97
Titus 3:4–7
Luke 2:15–20

Day

Isaiah 52:7–10
  Psalm 98
Hebrews 1:1–6
John 1:1–18

Christmas Day requires our best efforts at hospitality. Many parishes prepare a handout to welcome the many people who come to worship on this day. The handout can include prayers, songs or blessings for use at home. Extra copies of the schedule of services for the entire season might be available for visitors.

Other art for Christmas Day can be found on pages 6, 10 and 11.

Sunday in the Octave of Christmas

white

Feast of the Holy Family

Sirach 3:2–6, 12–14
  Psalm 128
Colossians 3:12–21
Luke 2:22–40

During Year B these readings may be used:
Genesis 15:1–6; 21:1–3
Hebrews 11:8, 11–12, 17–19
Luke 2:22–40

About the art: Today's feast reiterates the message of Christmas: God's holy one dwells among and within human life. Don't exclude anyone today by including only stereotyped images—either verbal or written—of families. Another image of today's gospel appears on page 17.

Note the images of St. Stephen, the first martyr (December 26), the Holy Innocents (December 28) and two of God's chosen ones, clothed in the rich garments of love, kindness, humility, meekness and patience.

Octave of Christmas

white

Mary, Mother of God

Numbers 6:22–27
   Psalm 67
Galatians 4:4–7
Luke 2:16–21

January 1, the Octave of Christmas, has many titles. On the Gregorian calendar, which most of the Western world follows, it is New Year's Day. On the Roman Catholic calendar, this day is "Mary, Mother of God," restoring the oldest Christian tradition of this day being kept as a feast of Mary. (The illustration of Mary and the Child on page 11 may be particularly appropriate.) The day also has been named World Day of Prayer for Peace. In the Byzantine calendar, January 1 is the Circumcision of the Lord (the title in the Roman calendar before it was reformed after Vatican II). In the Lutheran and Episcopalian calendars, the day is the feast of the Holy Name of Jesus.

About the art: In the first reading, Aaron blesses the Israelites. The gospel tells of the shepherds' visit to the child in the manger. In Galatians, Paul reminds us that because we have received the Spirit of Jesus, we can cry out to God, our Father. See page 46 for an illustration of the second reading.

Basil the Great and Gregory Nazianzen, bishops, scholars and friends, are celebrated on January 2. Two American citizens are remembered in this season as saints of the church: Elizabeth Ann Seton (January 4) and John Neumann (January 5).

Epiphany of the Lord

white

Isaiah 60:1–6
    Psalm 72
Ephesians 3:2–3a, 5–6
Matthew 2:1–12

Epiphany's traditional date is January 6, and many Christians throughout the world keep it on that date. In many Christian cultures, Epiphany is the day of gift-giving.

About the art: Epiphany means "revelation." Originally, the day celebrated many revelations of who Jesus is: his incarnation; his birth; his manifestations to the Magi, to the people gathered at the Jordan when Jesus was baptized by John (see page 12), and to the wedding guests at Cana.

One tradition observed today is the blessing of the home. (Many schools and other church institutions observe this custom, too.) The door to the home is marked in chalk with the cross, the year and the initials of the traditional names for the three kings: Caspar, Melchior and Balthasar. The text for this blessing can be found in *Catholic Household Blessings and Prayers.*

A tradition for many celebrations, the piñata, is illustrated on page 15.

Baptism of the Lord

white

Isaiah 42:1–4, 6–7
Psalm 29
Acts 10:34–38
Mark 1:7–11

During Year B these readings may be used:
Isaiah 55:1–11
1 John 5:1–9
Mark 1:7–11

About the art: The prophet Isaiah speaks of the one whom the Lord has called to bring prisioners out of confinement. Peter preaches to Cornelius and his household. Jesus is baptized by John and revealed as God's favored one.

This feast is a continuation of Epiphany and the conclusion to the Christmas season. Images of light and darkness, so prominent throughout this season, continue, and they are combined with baptismal images of water. Much of the art presented for today is also appropriate for celebrations of baptism.

St. Thomas Aquinas is remembered on January 28.

THIS IS MY BELOVED

AQUINAS

13

Winter Bulletin Cover

About the art: The gospels at Sunday Mass during the segment of Ordinary Time between Christmas and Lent in Year B are mostly from the beginning of Mark. These readings recount Jesus' preaching and healing. The second readings for the Second to the Sixth Sunday are all from 1 Corinthians, which is illustrated on page 14.

ORDINARY time

Second Sunday in Ordinary Time

green

1 Samuel 3:3b–10, 19
  Psalm 40
1 Corinthians 6:13c–15a, 17–20
John 1:35–42

About the art: Young Samuel hears the voice of the Lord for the first time. Two disciples hear Jesus' invitation to "Come and see."

The art in the lower left-hand corner of this page can be used to illustrate the readings from the First Letter of Paul to the Corinthians, which will be read on the Second through Sixth Sundays in Ordinary Time.

St. Anthony of Egypt (January 14) was one of the first "desert fathers." St. Agnes (January 21) was martyred in Rome about the year 300. Her name *(agna)* means "lamb" in Latin and "pure one" *(agne)* in Greek. Art for the Martin Luther King, Jr., holiday is on page 83.

LOOK THERE IS THE LAMB OF GOD

1 CORINTHIANS

15

Third Sunday in Ordinary Time

green

Jonah 3:1–5, 10
  Psalm 25
 1 Corinthians 7:29–31
Mark 1:14–20

About the art: God saves the great city of Nineveh through the preaching of the reluctant prophet, Jonah. Jesus calls Simon and Andrew to fish for people. For an illustration of the second reading, see page 14.

Pictures of wintertime activities can be used throughout the season. The border of musicians is useful throughout the year, as is the piñata party.

NINEVEH

Fourth Sunday in Ordinary Time

green

Deuteronomy 18:15–20
Psalm 95
1 Corinthians 7:32–35
Mark 1:21–28

About the art: Through Moses, God promises to raise up a prophet from among the Israelites. The psalm reminds us that God is our shepherd, just as God was a shepherd for the people in the desert. Jesus silences a shrieking, unclean spirit and casts it out of a man. For an illustration of the second reading, see page 14.

Presentation of the Lord

white

Malachi 3:1 – 4
Psalm 24
Hebrews 2:14 – 18
Luke 2:22 – 40

About the art: In accordance with Jewish law, Jesus was presented in the Temple 40 days after his birth, and two doves were sacrificed. For a rendering of the prophets Simeon and Anna, see page 6.

On this day, also called Candlemas, candles are blessed to acclaim Christ, the light of the world.

The church remembers St. Blaise (February 3), a bishop and martyr, mostly for his healing of a young boy who had a fish bone caught in his throat. Many communities celebrate the blessing of throats on this day.

BLAiSE

18

Fifth Sunday in Ordinary Time

green

Job 7:1–4, 6–7
  Psalm 147
  1 Corinthians 9:16–19, 22–23
Mark 1:29–39

About the art: Job laments the drudgery of human life. Jesus cures Simon's mother-in-law and soon finds himself sought by so many people in need of healing that, in order to have time to pray, he must get up early and go out to the desert. For an illustration of the second reading, see page 14.

St. Scholastica (February 10) was a woman of deep prayer and great love. She was the sister and follower of St. Benedict and the founder of the Benedictine women's communities.

St. Agatha (February 5) was a Roman Christian who was martyred in the fourth century. During her martyrdom, her breasts were cut off. Some have suggested that she can serve as a patron of women with breast cancer. If the parish has a cancer support group, perhaps they would like to use her image on their materials.

Art for Lincoln's Birthday is on page 83.

SCHOLASTICA

AGATHA

Sixth Sunday in Ordinary Time

green

Leviticus 13:1–2, 44–46
Psalm 32
1 Corinthians 10:31—11:1
Mark 1:40–45

About the art: Leviticus directs that those who are unclean must be brought before the priest. A leper presents himself to Jesus and is healed. For an illustration of the second reading, see page 14.

St. Valentine, a priest whose life is obscured by legend, is remembered in the culture as the patron of love on February 14. On the church's calendar, that day belongs to Cyril and Methodius, a monk and a bishop, respectively; they were brothers who ministered in what is now Slovakia and the Czech Republic.

Art for the national holidays in February is on page 83.

20

Seventh Sunday in Ordinary Time

green

Isaiah 43:18–19, 21–22, 24–25
  Psalm 41
2 Corinthians 1:18–22
Mark 2:1–12

About the art: The action of the Lord springs forth, like a river in a desert wasteland. Jesus heals the body as a sign of the forgiveness of sin, and still some people grumble.

The illustration in the upper right-hand corner is suitable for use whenever the Second Letter to the Corinthians is proclaimed. Another piece may be found on page 54.

Persons with disabilites are active, contributing members of church and society. Don't exclude them from the church's ministry or from its imagery.

21

Eighth Sunday in Ordinary Time

green

Hosea 2:16, 17, 21–22
    Psalm 103
2 Corinthians 3:1–6
Mark 2:18–22

About the art: The Lord speaks to Israel's heart, and the two are espoused in love and mercy. Paul tells us that we are Christ's letter, his word, written not in ink but in the Spirit. Jesus tells us that no one sews an unshrunken patch on an old piece of clothing, or pours new wine in an old wineskin.

The image of a father and child can be as powerful a sign of divine and human love as the image of a mother and child.

See pages 20 and 54 for art for the second reading.

22

Ninth Sunday in Ordinary Time

green

Deuteronomy 5:12–15
   Psalm 81
2 Corinthians 4:6–11
Mark 2:23—3:6

About the art: After his disciples are accused of violating the Sabbath by plucking some grain, Jesus reminds his listeners that the Sabbath is for the benefit of people. Then he heals a man with a withered hand. Paul reminds us that we possess in earthen vessels the treasure of God's glory in Jesus Christ. Psalm 81 states that when Joseph (of the many-colored coat—a symbol of all Israel) came forth from the land of Egypt, God decreed that Israel should sing.

Carnival masks remind us that Lent is coming soon.

See pages 20 and 54 for art for the second reading.

23

Lent Bulletin Cover

Lent lasts from Ash Wednesday until the celebration of the Evening Mass of the Lord's Supper on Holy Thursday.

Lent is a time for catechumens to prepare to make the promises of baptism at Easter and for the whole community to renew them. The heart of this preparation is the threefold discipline of prayer, fasting and almsgiving.

LENT

Ash Wednesday

violet

Joel 2:12–18
   Psalm 51
2 Corinthians 5:20—6:2
Matthew 6:1–6, 16–18

About the art: "Proclaim a fast," today's scriptures demand, and so we do. We begin Lent with a reminder to return to the Lord, just as the people of Israel did with prayers and sacrifices. Jesus reminds us that our prayer, fasting and almsgiving must be done simply, not as a show for others.

See pages 20 and 54 for art for the second reading.

25

First Sunday of Lent

violet

Genesis 9:8–15
Psalm 25
I Peter 3:18–22
Mark 1:12–15

About the art: Noah and his family and a few select animals find refuge in the ark from destruction. Afterward, God promises never again to destroy creation through water. The ark is also a symbol of the church, saved through the deadly, life-giving waters of baptism. After his own baptism, Jesus is led into the desert by the Spirit. There he is tempted by the devil and ministered to by angels.

Some of these images are appropriate for the Easter Vigil and throughout the Easter season.

26

Second Sunday of Lent

violet

Genesis 22:1–2, 9a, 10–13, 15–18
Psalm 116
Romans 8:31b–34
Mark 9:2–9

About the art: Abraham was obedient to God, even to the point of being willing to sacrifice his beloved son Isaac. (See page 47 for another image of the sacrifice of Isaac.) Because Jesus was obedient, he was raised and sits at God's right hand. The glory of the risen Lord—and of all the baptized—is foreseen in his transfiguration before the disciples. (See page 59 for another image of the transfiguration.)

DO NOT TELL ANYONE

27

Third Sunday of Lent

violet

Exodus 20:1–17
   Psalm 19
1 Corinthians 1:22–25
John 2:13–25

The readings of Year A may be used on this Sunday, especially when the scrutinies are celebrated:
Exodus 17:3–7
   Psalm 94
Romans 5:1–2, 5–8
John 4:5–42

About the art: As a sign of the covenant, the Lord gives Israel the Ten Commandments. Jesus rails against those who turn religion into commerce, and he predicts his own death and resurrection.

Perpetua and Felicity (March 7), two Roman women of different rank, lived and died as sisters in Christ during the time of the Roman persecutions.

28

Fourth Sunday of Lent

violet or rose

2 Chronicles 36:14–17, 19–23
    Psalm 137
Ephesians 2:4–10
John 3:14–21

*The readings of Year A may be used on this Sunday,
especially when the scrutinies are celebrated:*
1 Samuel 16:1, 6–7, 10–13
    Psalm 23
Ephesians 5:8–14
John 9:1–41

About the art: After losing the battle with the Chaldeans, the Israelites are taken into exile in Babylon, where, the psalms say, they hang up their harps, too dejected to sing the songs of Zion. Jeremiah stirs up the king, Cyrus, who frees the Israelites and builds a temple for them in Jerusalem. Jesus teaches Nicodemus about eternal life and light.

The border presents some of saints of the season.

MAY GOD

BE WITH YOU

29

Fifth Sunday of Lent

violet

Jeremiah 31:31—34
   Psalm 51
Hebrews 5:7—9
John 12:20—33

The readings of Year A may be used on this Sunday, especially when the scrutinies are celebrated.
Ezekiel 37:12—14
   Psalm 130
Romans 8:8—11
John 11:1—45

About the art: Through Jeremiah, the Lord promises to plant a new law in the hearts of the people. Jesus' example of the wheat that dies to bear great fruit foreshadows his glorification through suffering, death and resurrection. A voice from heaven (or was it thunder?) promises that God's name will be glorified again.

30

Passion (Palm) Sunday

red

Procession:
>   *Mark 11:1–10*
>   *or John 12:12–16*

Isaiah 50:4–7
>   *Psalm 22*
Philippians 2:6–11
Mark 14:1—15:47

About the art: The events we remember on Palm Sunday—Jesus' triumphal entry into Jerusalem, a woman washing Jesus' feet and anointing his head, Jesus' trial, torture, death and burial—are a profound meditation on Jesus' life, and on the meaning of life for all who would follow him.

31

Triduum Bulletin Cover

The Paschal Triduum of the death, burial and resurrection of the Lord lasts from the celebration of the Mass of the Lord's Supper on Holy Thursday until Easter Sunday sundown.

About the art: Through his death and resurrection Christ has conquered sin and death. IC XC NIKA is Greek for "Jesus Christ, victor."

INRI

IC·XC·NI·KA

TRIDUM

Holy Thursday Evening

white

Exodus 12:1–8, 11–14
   Psalm 116
1 Corinthians 11:23–26
John 13:1–15

About the art: On Holy Thursday (or at some earlier time) the bishop gathers with the clergy and laity to prepare the oils for the celebration of the sacraments throughout the coming year, especially for the celebrations of baptism and confirmation at Easter. Many parishes incorporate the receiving of the oils into the Mass of the Lord's Supper.

This evening the story of the Passover of the Jews from slavery to freedom begins the telling of the story of Jesus' Passover—and ours—from death to life, which we celebrate throughout the Triduum.

During the period of adoration following this evening's Mass, many parishes read the account of Jesus in the Garden of Gethsemani.

See pages 29 and 47 for other images for today.

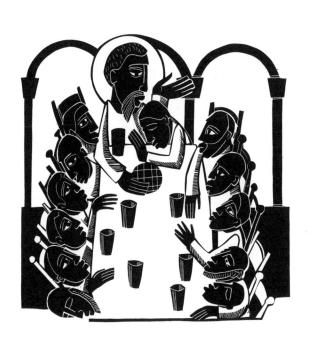

Good Friday

red

Isaiah 52:13—53:12
Psalm 31
Hebrews 4:14—16, 5:7—9
John 18:1—19:42

About the art: Today we remember and venerate the cross of Jesus, the suffering servant of God. Other images of the cross and passion of Christ are on pages 27, 29, 30, 50, 64 and 67.

Easter Vigil

white

Genesis 1:1—2:2
   Psalm 104
   or Psalm 33
Genesis 22:1–18
   Psalm 16
Exodus 14:15—15:1
   Exodus 15
Isaiah 54:5–14
   Psalm 30
Isaiah 55:1–11
   Isaiah 12
   or Psalm 51

Baruch 3:9–15, 32—4:4
   Psalm 19:8–11
Ezekiel 36:16–28
   Psalms 42 and 43
   or Isaiah 12
   or Psalm 51
Romans 6:3–11
   Psalm 118
Matthew 28:1–10

About the art: The story of God's relationship to human-kind is retold this night, from the creation to the resurrection, to our own death and resurrection in the waters of baptism.

Other images of Adam and Eve can be found on pages 48 and 71. More art appropriate for the Easter Vigil can be found on page 25.

YOU NEED NOT BE AMAZED. HE IS NOT HERE.

Easter Season Bulletin Cover

The Easter season lasts from Easter Sunday until Pentecost Sunday.

About the art: In the outpouring of the Holy Spirit, the disorder brought down upon Babel is restored to order, and the covenant of Moses is fulfilled.

EASTER.

Easter Sunday

white

Acts 10:34a, 37–43
    Psalm 118
Colossians 3:1–4
    or *1 Corinthians 5:6b–8*
John 20:1–9
    or *Matthew 16:1–7*
    or *Luke 24:13–35 (evening Mass)*

About the art: "The stone which the builders rejected has become the cornerstone," proclaims Psalm 118, the great Easter psalm. The great joy of Mary Magdalene, Peter and the other apostles spills out into the preaching of the good news.

37

Second Sunday of Easter

white

Acts 4:32–35
  Psalm 118
1 John 5:1–6
John 20:19–31

About the art: Thomas comes to believe by touching the wounded, risen body of Christ. Through faith in him, John tells us, we are children of God. The early Christians expressed their faith through the sharing of their goods among all.

A generic image for all the Sundays on which readings from the First Letter of John are proclaimed is found on page 40.

The martyr George (April 23) is remembered as one who slew a dragon, another image of the conquest of sin. Catherine of Siena (April 29), mystic and doctor of the church, wrote on the mystery of the cross and urged the pope to move from Avignon to Rome.

Third Sunday of Easter

white

Acts 3:13–15, 17–19
  Psalm 4
1 John 2:1–5a
Luke 24:35–48

About the art: The Risen Lord appears to those gathered in the upper room. Mark, the predominant evangelist in Year B, is symbolized as a lion.

Generic art for the second reading is on page 40.

Fourth Sunday of Easter

white

Acts 4:8–12
  Psalm 118
1 John 3:1–2
John 10:11–18

About the art: Today sometimes is called Good Shepherd Sunday because the gospel readings for the Fourth Sunday of Easter, always from John, deal with shepherds and sheep. In the first reading, Peter declares that the crippled man who was healed was made whole by the name of Jesus, the cornerstone. The First Letter of John asserts that by love we are God's children.

Generic art for the second reading is found on page 40.

40

Fifth Sunday of Easter

white

Acts 9:26–31
  Psalm 22
1 John 3:18–24
John 15:1–8

About the art: Through the testimony of Barnabas, Saul (Paul) was accepted in Jerusalem by the disciples of Jesus, whom he had previously persecuted, and he begins to preach boldly. Jesus is the true vine without whom we can do nothing. Psalm 22 declares, "To him alone shall bow down all who sleep in the earth."

Sixth Sunday of Easter

white

Acts 10:25–26, 34–35, 44–48
  Psalm 98
1 John 4:7–10
John 15:9–17

About the art: Nine times Jesus uses the word "love" in today's gospel. As he has loved them, so they are to love. The First Letter of John reaffirms the message. In the first reading, Peter meets Cornelius and preaches on the wideness of God's love.

A generic image for the second reading appears on page 40.

Isidore (May 15) was a poor Spanish farmer. In Spain, his wife, Maria Torribia, is also regarded as a saint. They were renowned for their devotion to prayer and for their generosity to the poor, even though they were poor themselves. Isidore is the patron of farmers.

MARIA

TORRIBIA

ISIDORE

42

Ascension of the Lord

white

Acts 1:1–11
  Psalm 47
Ephesians 1:17–23
  or Ephesians 4:1–13
Mark 16:15–20

About the art: Jesus commissions the Eleven to make disciples of all nations and to baptize them. Then he ascends to his place at God's right hand, where he reigns in majesty over all the earth.

ALLELUiA

PEOPLE

WHY DO YOU LOOK TO THE SKIES

43

Seventh Sunday of Easter

white

Acts 1:15–17, 20a, 20c–26
  Psalm 103
1 John 4:11–16
John 17:11b–19

In Canada, this Sunday is observed as the Solemnity of the Ascension of the Lord.

About the art: Jesus prays that his Father will protect and sanctify his disciples. After Jesus' Ascension, the community and the Lord chose Matthias to take the place of Judas. Psalm 103 exhorts everyone, including the angels, to bless the Lord.

Generic art for the second reading can be found on page 40.

44

Pentecost

red

Vigil

Genesis 11:1–9
   or *Exodus 19:3–8, 16–20*
   or *Ezekiel 37:1–4*
   or *Joel 3:1–5*
   Psalm 104
Romans 8:22–27
John 7:37–39

Day

Acts 2:1–11
   Psalm 104
1 Corinthians 12:3–7, 12–13
   or *Galatians 5:16–25*
John 20:19–23

About the art: In the readings of the vigil, the presumption of those who would build a tower to the heavens prompts the Lord to send the chaos of many languages; Ezekiel prophesies to the dry bone, and the spirit comes into them; God promises to pour out God's spirit on all people, and to work many wonders such as the sun turning dark and the moon turning to blood. On Pentecost day, the Spirit is poured out like fire on those gathered, and they begin to prophesy.

45

Summer Bulletin Cover

Ordinary Time—"counted" time—resumes with evening prayer on Pentecost Sunday, but two Sunday feasts, Trinity Sunday and the Solemnity of the Body and Blood of Christ, occur before we settle into the long green period. In Year B, when most of the Sunday gospel readings are taken from the Gospel of Mark, five Sundays—the Seventeenth to the Twenty-first—are devoted to the "Bread of Life" readings from the Gospel of John.

In the Northern hemisphere, Ordinary Time resumes in the late spring, and the summer months are filled with signs of life (crops in the fields and orchards, children and families at play) and death (floods and drought, holiday traffic deaths, urban violence). During this time the church remembers the lives and deaths of John the Baptist, of St. Peter and St. Paul, of Mary the Mother of Jesus and, at every eucharist, of Jesus. The memory of the cross of Christ is celebrated in a special way on the feast of the Triumph of the Holy Cross on September 14, about the time that summer begins to turn to autumn.

ORDINARY TIME

46

Trinity Sunday

white

Deuteronomy 4:32–34, 39–40
   Psalm 33
Romans 8:14–17
Mark 28:16–20

About the art: Moses asks the people if any god ever did what the Lord has done for them. Paul reminds the Romans that the spirit they received was a spirit of adoption through which God's children may cry, "Abba!" Jesus commissions the disciples to baptize all nations in the name of the triune God, and he promises to be with them always.

The shamrock is a symbol of the Trinity; the wall flower is a symbol of faithfulness.

47

Body and Blood of Christ

white

Exodus 24:3–8
  Psalm 147
Hebrews 9:11–15
Mark 14:12–16, 22–26

About the art: The people of Israel offer sacrifice to God, and Moses pours the blood of the sacrifices on the altar. In the sequence, the sacrifice of Isaac is linked to that of Christ. In the gospel Jesus declares, "If you do not eat of the flesh of the Son of Man, and drink his blood, you have no life in you."

Charles Lwanga and his companions (June 3) were martyred in Uganda in the nineteenth century for preaching the gospel. Boniface (June 5), who brought the faith to Germany in the eighth century, suffered the same fate.

The art here is also useful for first communions and for Holy Thursday.

BONIFACE

CHARLES LWANGA

48

Tenth Sunday in Ordinary Time

green

Genesis 3:9–15
Psalm 130
2 Corinthians 4:13 — 5:1
Mark 3:20–35

About the art: Adam and Eve each pass the blame for their sin on to another. Jesus' relatives arrive when he is preaching, and he declares, "Whoever does the will of God is brother and sister and mother to me." Paul encourages the Corinthians not to be concerned for this earthly tent, for there is a dwelling for us provided by God. Psalm 130 exhorts, "More than sentinels wait for the dawn, let Israel wait for the Lord."

Irenaeus (July 28) was bishop of Lyons and a martyr for the faith in the second century. His name means "peacemaker." The border illustrates the corporal works of mercy.

See pages 20 and 54 for art for the second reading.

IRENÆUS

49

Eleventh Sunday in Ordinary Time

green

Ezekiel 17:22–24
    Psalm 92
2 Corinthians 5:6–10
Mark 4:26–34

About the art: Through Ezekiel, God promises to take the tender twig of Israel and make of it a great cedar. Jesus says that the reign of God is like a field that grows. When the grain is ripe, the sower takes a sickle, for the harvest has come. The reign of God is like a tiny mustard seed from which God creates a sturdy shrub that provides shelter for birds.

See pages 20 and 54 for art for the second reading.

50

Twelfth Sunday in Ordinary Time

green

Job 38:1, 8–11
   Psalm 107
2 Corinthians 5:14–17
Mark 4:35–40

About the art: God speaks to Job from the whirlwind. Jesus calms the storm, but not until it has stirred up the disciples. Paul tells the Corinthians that anyone who is in Christ is a new creation.

See pages 20 and 54 for art for the second reading.

Birth of John the Baptist

white

Vigil

Jeremiah 1:4—10

Psalm 71

1 Peter 1:8—12

Luke 1:5—17

Day

Isaiah 49:1—6

Psalm 139

Acts 13:22—26

Luke 1:57—66, 80

About the art: Jeremiah receives the word of God. Zachary, the father of John the Baptist, offers incense in the sanctuary, where the angel speaks to him. Like John, Isaiah was a sharp-edged sword and a polished arrow.

HIS NAME IS JOHN

52

Thirteenth Sunday in Ordinary Time

green

Wisdom 1:13–15; 2:23–24
  Psalm 30
2 Corinthians 8:7, 9, 13–15
Mark 5:21–43

About the art: God created all things, the Book of Wisdom says, and does not delight in their death. Jesus raises the daughter of Jairus from the dead and heals the woman afflicted with a hemorrhage. Paul exhorts the Corinthians to share their excess so that none should want.

The border illustrates the spiritual works of mercy.

See pages 20 and 54 for art for the second reading.

53

Peter and Paul

red

Vigil
Acts 3:1–10
   Psalm 19:2–5
Galatians 1:11–20
John 21:15–19

Day
Acts 12:1–11
   Psalm 34
2 Timothy 4:6–8, 17–18
Matthew 16:13–19

About the art: Peter and John offer the crippled man what they can—healing in the name of Jesus Christ. Peter is rescued from jail by an angel. Paul, poured out like a libation, awaits the crown of victory. Jesus commands Peter to feed his sheep. As in Psalm 19, the heavens declare the glory of God.

Illustrations for Independence Day and other national days are on page 83.

54

Fourteenth Sunday in Ordinary Time

green

Ezekiel 2:2–5
   Psalm 123
2 Corinthians 12:7–10
Mark 6:1–6

About the art: The spirit of God sets Ezekiel on his feet and sends him to prophesy to Israel. Jesus teaches in the synagogue in his own village, but the people found his teaching difficult to accept. Paul writes of the "thorn in the flesh" given to him that he might not become too proud. Psalm 123 proclaims that our eyes are fixed on the Lord as the eyes of a maid are on the hands of her mistress.

See page 20 for another piece of art for the reading from 2 Corinthians.

The apostle Thomas (July 3) is remembered as the one who doubted, but he spread the gospel to India and died there for the faith.

Illustrations for Independence Day and other national days are on page 83.

THO
MAS

II
CORINTHIANS

Fifteenth Sunday in Ordinary Time

green

Amos 7:12–15
   Psalm 85
Ephesians 1:3–14
Mark 6:7–13

About the art: Amos, the shepherd and dresser of syc-amores, becomes a prophet at the Lord's command. Jesus sends the Twelve to preach repentance. Through them, God's plan to bring all things under Christ's head-ship will be carried out.

Benedict (July 11) is considered the father of Western monasticism. His rule directed that monastic life should balance work and prayer, and that monasteries should be places of hospitality.

Kateri Tekakwitha (July 14), born in the area that is now part of New York, was a woman of the Mohawk nation. She became a catechumen and was baptized at the age of 20. She lived in a Christian Mohawk community near Montreal until she died at the age of 24.

Mary Magdalene (July 22), the "apostle to the apostles," followed Jesus to his death and was the first to pro-claim his resurrection.

A generic image for the second reading is found on page 56.

56

Sixteenth Sunday in Ordinary Time

green

Jeremiah 23:1–6
　Psalm 23
Ephesians 2:13–18
Mark 6:30–34

About the art: Jesus and the apostles go off in the boat to find a place to rest, but the crowds follow. Jesus begins to teach them, for they are like sheep without a shepherd. The image in the upper right hand corner may be used for all the Sundays on which the Letter to the Ephesians is proclaimed.

EPHESIAN S

DAVID

57

Seventeenth Sunday in Ordinary Time

green

2 Kings 4:42–44
Psalm 145
Ephesians 4:1–6
John 6:1–15

About the art: The prophet Elisha feeds 100 people with 20 barley loaves. After going up to the mountain to be alone with the disciples, Jesus feeds 5,000 people with five loaves and two fish. Psalm 145 gives praise to God, who satisfies the desires of all creatures.

From this Sunday until the Twenty-first Sunday in Ordinary Time, the gospels are taken from the "bread of life" passages in the Gospel of John. Appropriate art can be found throughout this section.

A generic image for the second reading is found on page 56.

58

Eighteenth Sunday in Ordinary Time

green

Exodus 16:2–4, 12–15
  Psalm 78
Ephesians 4:17, 20–24
John 6:24–35

About the art: The Lord sends quail and manna to feed the Israelites in the desert. Jesus is the bread of life. Paul tells the Ephesians that they must put on a new way of thinking and become new people in Christ.

A generic image for the second reading is found on page 56.

59

Transfiguration of the Lord

white

Daniel 7:9–10, 13–14
  Psalm 97
2 Peter 1:16–19
Mark 9:2–10

About the art: The prophet Daniel has a vision of the Ancient One on the throne and of the son of man receiving dominion, glory and kingship. Jesus is transformed before Peter, James and John, and takes his place with Moses and Elijah. The Second Letter of Peter says we should attend to the message, "This is my beloved Son," as we would to a lamp in the darkness.

For other appropriate art for this day, see page 26.

LISTEN TO HIM

60

Nineteenth Sunday in Ordinary Time

green

1 Kings 19:4–8
  Psalm 34
Ephesians 4:30—5:2
John 6:41–51

About the art: Elijah prays for death, but instead is given food in the desert. To those who protest, Jesus asserts that he truly is the bread of life. Paul exhorts the Ephesians to be kind, compassionate and forgiving.

Dominic (August 8) was a priest who founded the Dominicans to preach the truth in the face of heresy. Clare of Assisi (August 11) was a companion of Francis and the founder of the women's Franciscan community. Her name means "light."

DO
MI
NI
C

CLARE

61

Assumption of Mary, August 15

white

Vigil

1 Chronicles 15:3–4, 15, 16;
16:1–2
Psalm 132
1 Corinthians 15:54–57
Luke 11:27–28

Day

Revelation 11:19;
12:1–6, 10
Psalm 45
1 Corinthians 15:20–26
Luke 1:39–56

About the art: The feast of the Annunciation recalls many images of Mary: the maiden visited by an angel; the young pregnant woman visiting her older, pregnant cousin; the woman clothed with the sun, a sign in opposition to the seven-headed dragon; the Ark of the Covenant that bore God's word; the faithful believer who shares in Christ's victory over death.

62

Twentieth Sunday in Ordinary Time

green

Proverbs 9:1–6
Psalm 34
Ephesians 5:15–20
John 6:51–58

About the art: Wisdom invites all to her table. Jesus invites all to partake of the living bread. Those who are filled with the Spirit will address each other with psalms and hymns and inspired songs. The blue bonnet is a symbol of hunger; the walnut tree is a symbol of wisdom.

Bernard of Clairvaux (August 20), a twelfth-century abbot, was a preacher against heresy, an advisor to popes and a reformer of monasticism. Monica (August 27) was a mother through whose prayers and pleading her pagan son Augustine became a Christian.

AUGUS
TINE

MONI
CA

BERNARD

63

Twenty-first Sunday in Ordinary Time

green

Joshua 24:1–2a, 15–17, 18b
  Psalm 34
Ephesians 5:2a, 25–32
  or Ephesians 5:21–32
John 6:60–69

About the art: Joshua offers the Israelites the freedom
to choose whom they will serve. When many disciples
leave because they cannot endure his teaching, Jesus
asks the Twelve if they, too, will go. Paul teaches that
husbands must love their wives as Christ loves the
church. Psalm 34 assures us that the Lord hears the
cries of the just.

64

Twenty-second Sunday in Ordinary Time

green

Deuteronomy 4:1−2, 6−8
   Psalm 15
James 1:17−18, 21b−22, 27
Mark 7:1−8, 14−15, 21−23

About the art: Moses enjoins Israel to follow the command of the Lord. Jesus argues with the scholars over their disregard of God's law and their insistence upon following human tradition. James directs his community to take care of widows and orphans.

Art appropriate for all the Sundays on which the Letter of James is proclaimed can be found on page 70.

On August 29, the church remembers the beheading of John the Baptist. Gregory the Great (September 3) was a brilliant and wise pope and teacher. Peter Claver (September 9) was a priest who spent most of his life serving black slaves in Colombia.

GREGORY

PETER CLAVER

65

Twenty-third Sunday in Ordinary Time

green

Isaiah 35:4–7a
Psalm 146
James 2:1–5
Mark 7:31–37

About the art: When the Lord comes, the blind will see, the deaf will hear, the lame will leap like a stag, the mute will speak, the sands of the desert will become pools of water. Psalm 146 adds that the Lord sets captives free. Jesus cures a deaf man. James warns Christians not to show favoritism to the rich and powerful.

Art appropriate for all the Sundays on which James is proclaimed can be found on page 70.

66

Twenty-fourth Sunday in Ordinary Time

green

Isaiah 50:4–9a
Psalm 116
James 2:14–18
Mark 8:27–35

About the art: Although he is beaten and reviled, the servant of the Lord is not disgraced. Jesus tells the disciples that he must suffer, to which Peter reacts negatively. Jesus reprimands Peter for judging by human standards. James directs the community to put their faith into action.

Art appropriate for all the Sundays on which James is proclaimed can be found on page 70.

Cornelius, a pope, and Cyprian, a bishop, were good and holy pastors in the third century. They died as martyrs and are remembered on September 16.

CYP
RIAN

COR
NEL
IUS

67

Triumph of the Cross

white

Numbers 21:4–9
Psalm 78
Philippians 2:6–11
John 3:13–17

About the art: Today's feast evokes many images of the cross: a glorious, jeweled cross; an Ethiopian cross; a cross from which springs life-giving water. The saving cross of Christ is prefigured by the serpent mounted on the pole, which saved the Israelites from death by snakebite in the desert.

John Chrysostom (September 13) was an eloquent preacher and prolific writer who was patriarch of Constantinople. He was sent into exile by the empress, and died of the rigors of the journey in 407.

The feast of Our Lady of Sorrows (September 15) focuses on the human suffering of the cross, in contrast with the focus on the glory of the cross on September 14.

CHRYSOSTOM

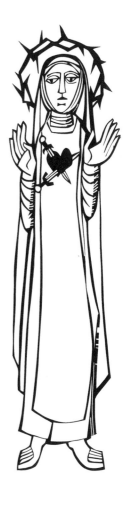

68

Autumn Bulletin Cover

Ordinary Time continues through the autumn, as we settle back into the routines of work and school, as the days grow shorter and colder, as the green fields turn gold and then brown. Our thoughts turn to our own end. We celebrate Halloween to look in the face of death and fear, and laugh. In Mexican communities, the *Día de los Muertos* reminds us that death is part of life and that the dead are still with the living, as the living will one day be with the dead. As Christians, we remember our beloved dead, especially at the beginning of November, and all month we look forward in faith to the time when everything we know will come to an end and Christ will reign in the fullness of God's kingdom.

ORDINARY time

69

Twenty-fifth Sunday in Ordinary Time

green

Wisdom 2:17–20
Psalm 54
James 3:16—4:3
Mark 9:29–37

About the art: In the Book of Wisdom, the wicked people plot against the just person. After speaking of his impending death, Jesus teaches his disciples that they are to be servants of all, welcoming even the children. James writes, "The harvest of justice is sown in peace."

Art appropriate for all the Sundays on which James is proclaimed can be found on page 70.

Matthew (September 21), a tax collector, became an apostle, an evangelist, a missionary and a martyr.

70

Twenty-sixth Sunday in Ordinary Time

green

Nehemiah 11:25–29
  Psalm 19
James 5:1–6
Mark 9:38–43, 45, 47–48

About the art: Moses bestows on the elders some of the spirit that he had received, and they begin to prophesy. Jesus assures the disciples that anyone who does good in his name will be rewarded. James warns the rich that their ill-gotten wealth will decay, and so will they themselves. This art may be used for all the Sundays when the Letter of James is proclaimed.

The archangels Michael, Gabriel and Raphael (September 29) are celebrated as messengers, protectors, intercessors and companions. Uriel, often forgotten, also is pictured here.

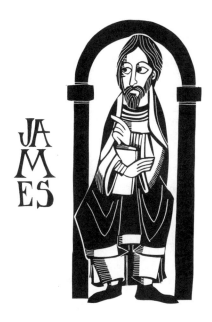

JAMES

MICH AEL

GA BR IEL

RAPH AEL

UR IEL

71

Twenty-seventh Sunday in Ordinary Time

green

Genesis 2:18–24
Psalm 128
Hebrews 2:9–11
Mark 10:2–16

About the art: God creates woman and man to have a relationship unique within creation. The psalm celebrates home life as a blessing—with children like olive plants around the table. Jesus affirms the sacredness of marriage, and he demands that children be allowed to come to him. The image of the book and sword is appropriate for all the Sundays on which the Letter to the Hebrews is proclaimed.

For an image of Our Lady of the Rosary (October 7), see page 74. Other images of Adam and Eve appear on pages 34 and 48.

HEBREWS

72

Twenty-eighth Sunday in Ordinary Time

green

Wisdom 7:7–11
Psalm 23
Hebrews 4:12–13
Mark 10:17–3

About the art: The author of the Book of Wisdom begs to be given wisdom, valuing it above scepter and throne. Jesus tells a man he must sell all he has and give the money to the poor. Afterward, he tells the disciples that it is easier for a camel to pass through a needle's eye (a narrow gate) than for a rich person to enter the reign of God.

For an illustration of the second reading, see page 71.

The Guardian Angels, protectors of all, are remembered on October 2. Francis of Assisi (October 4), founder of the Friars Minor, is known as the troubadour of divine love and friend to all creation. Teresa of Avila (October 15) was a mystic and a reformer of the Carmelite order. Her writings on the spiritual life are the foundation of the teachings of all later writers on the subject.

TERESA

OF AVILA

73

Twenty-ninth Sunday in Ordinary Time

green

Isaiah 53:10–11
Psalm 33
Hebrews 4:14–16
Mark 10:35–45

About the art: James and John request places of honor in the reign of God. Jesus teaches all the disciples that those who would be great must serve.

Ignatius (October 17), who was bishop of Antioch, was martyred during the persecution of Trajan in the early second century. The letters he wrote to his people on the way to his death express his longing to be united with Christ.

Art on this page is appropriate for morning and evening prayers. For an illustration of the second reading, see page 71.

MORNING PRAYER

IGNATIUS OF ANTIOCH

EVENING PRAYER

74

Thirtieth Sunday in Ordinary Time

green

Jeremiah 31:7–9
Psalm 126
Hebrews 5:1–6
Mark 10:46–52

About the art: Through Jeremiah, the Lord promises to return all of Israel—including the blind and the lame— to their own land. Psalm 126, referring to the capture of Zion, promises that they who sow in tears will reap in joy. Jesus cures Bartimaeus of his blindness. The Letter to the Hebrews contrasts Christ with earthly priests, who offer sacrifices for themselves and for the people. For a generic image of the second reading, see page 71.

The memorial of Our Lady of the Holy Rosary (October 7) honors Mary for the protection she affords the church. The date is the anniversary of the battle between Christians and Turks at Lepanto in 1571, which the Christians won after the rosary was recited.

JESUS SON OF DAVID HAVE PITY ON ME

75

Thirty-first Sunday in Ordinary Time

green

Deuteronomy 6:2–6
  Psalm 18
Hebrews 7:23–28
Mark 12:28b–34

About the art: Moses teaches the people the heart
of the law: to love God and neighbor. Jesus reaffirms
this teaching and approves of the scribe who notes
that this command is worth more than burnt offerings.
Psalm 18 praises God as rock, fortress, shield and
horn of salvation.

All Saints

white

Revelation 7:2–4, 9–14
   Psalm 24
1 John 3:1–3
Matthew 5:1–12

About the art: The feast of All Saints calls forth images of the end-time: the angel holding the seal with which to imprint the servants of God, the four horsemen of the apocalypse, the Lamb surrounded by angels and saints, the saints dressed in white. The palm branch is a symbol of the victory of the reign of God.

77

All Souls

black, violet or white

Readings for All Souls can draw from any of the readings for the Masses for the Dead.

About the art: The images of All Souls Day combine remembrance of the beloved dead with hope of their—and our—resurrection. Many parishes keep a book for the writing and remembering of the names of the dead. This book is often kept in the gathering space or near the baptismal font.

WHY DO YOU SEARCH FOR THE LIVING AMONG THE DEAD

78

Thirty-second Sunday in Ordinary Time

green

1 Kings 17:10–16
Psalm 146
Hebrews 9:24–28
Mark 12:38–44

About the art: The widow of Zarephath shares her last bit of flour and oil with the prophet Elijah, but the Lord feeds the widow, her son and Elijah for a year. Jesus rails against religious leaders who dress in finery and demand special treatment. He holds up the widow, who gives despite her need, as a model for those who would follow him.

Frances Xavier Cabrini (November 13) was an Italian immigrant who served the poor, especially in Chicago. She died in 1917 and was the first citizen of the United States to be canonized. Elizabeth of Hungary (November 17), daughter of a king and wife of a nobleman, lived a life of prayer and charity. After the death of her husband, she continued her work as a member of the Third Order of St. Francis.

79

Dedication of St. John Lateran

white

Any readings from the common for the dedication of a
church may be chosen.

About the art: This is the dedication anniversary of
the cathedral of Rome, the "mother church" of Roman
Catholics. Images drawn from the many options for
readings include Jacob's vision of a ladder of angels, the
ark of the covenant, the Temple of Jerusalem, an angel
carrying incense, and Jesus at the home of Zacchaeus.

TODAY SALVATION HAS COME TO THIS HOUSE

80

Thirty-third Sunday in Ordinary Time

green

Daniel 12:1—3
Psalm 16
Hebrews 10:11—14, 18
Mark 13:24—32

About the art: Michael, the guardian of the people, shall arise in a time of great distress. After the time of trial, Jesus foretells, the sun and the moon and the stars will all become dark, and the Son of Man will come in glory.

Rose Philippine Duchesne (November 18) was a Religious of the Sacred Heart of Jesus. She was French by birth, but came to the United States to teach and to serve the Native American people. She died in Missouri in 1852 and was canonized in 1988.

Andrew Dung-Lac and many other Vietnamese Christians (November 24) were martyred during the seventeenth, eighteenth and nineteenth centuries. Andrew and 116 others were canonized in 1988.

PHILIPPINE
DUCHESNE

ANDREW
DUNG LAC

81

Christic the King

white

Last Sunday in Ordinary Time

Daniel 7:13–14
Psalm 93
Revelation 1:5–8
John 18:33b–37

About the art: Psalm 93 proclaims, "The Lord is king, he is robed in majesty." Jesus responds to Pilate that his kingdom is not of this world. The Book of Revelation asserts that the Lord is Alpha and Omega.

Other images of Christ the King appear on page 42.

Thanksgiving Day

white

Readings may be chosen from the weekday; from the Masses for various public needs, "After the Harvest" or "In Thanksgiving"; or from the votive Mass for Thanksgiving Day.

About the art: Some of the images suggested by the readings include Solomon before the Temple, blessing God for the favors bestowed on Israel, and Jesus instructing the man who had been exorcised of a demon to go home and tell his family what the Lord had done for him.

Little is known for certain of the apostle Andrew (November 30), but tradition tells of his great love for the cross of Christ and of his own death on an X-shaped cross.

Dorothy Day was a journalist, a convert to the faith, an activist for the cause of justice and the co-founder (with Peter Maurin) of the Catholic Worker movement. She died on November 29, 1980.

DOROTHY DAY

83

National Days

Martin Luther King, Jr., Birthday
January 15,
observed on the third Monday in January

Lincoln's Birthday
February 12

Presidents' Day
Third Monday in February

Washington's Birthday
February 22

Victoria Day (Canada)
Third Monday in May

Memorial Day
Last Monday in May

Canada Day
July 1

Independence Day
July 4

Labor Day
First Monday in September

Columbus Day
October 12,
observed on the second Monday in October

Election Day (U.S.A.)
First Tuesday after the first Monday in November

Veteran's Day
November 11

Remembrance Day (Canada)
November 11

Index